Gazette

Gazette

Anthony Hassett

C S F Publishing

.

Paperback ISBN 978-1-937487-62-1
eBook ISBN 978-1-937487-61-4

Web: csfpublishing.com
Email: info@csfpublishing.com

to Erin...

Anthony Hassett, New Mexico. 2012

Anthony Hassett

Of Anthony Hassett's multiple incessant genius, he is best known in small quiet circles abroad for his humor, and known domestically for his oft-times caustic critiques in various art magazines. That of the poet, the painter, the cultural and political journalist, the philosopher, can be glimpsed for the first time in this dynamic volume that is at once boldly public and profoundly personal, and that combines Hassett's powerful poetic voice with his equally powerful renderer's hand.

As an "angel-headed" adolescent, Hassett was among the first disciples of the Beats: the mid-century writers and artists whose work shared themes of spirituality, environmental awareness, and political dissidence. He left Venice Beach at the age of fifteen with his thumb pointing skyward. By the time he reached the classrooms of William S. Burroughs and Allen Ginsberg at Naropa Institute in Boulder, Hassett's early life was already one of uncompromised nonconformity, intentional obscurity, and above all, radiant poetry. His life continues to embody Marcuse' "Great Refusal", and has found him variously in jail cells with infamous political dissidents; in the salons of Nepalese poets and photographers; deported from Morocco; arrested in Athens; in detention by British military in caves beneath the Rock of Gibraltar; at dinner tables with famed writers and filmmakers in Rome, Paris, Istanbul, NY, and LA; and on the sofas of Sandinistas, Chavistas, Panthers, and Weather Underground; at a porn theatre on Christmas Eve in New Jersey; in Copacabana, Bolivia on the Day of the Dead; in riots in Chile; at Marxist-Lacanian conferences in Berlin; in confinement in Frankfurt during the Chernobyl meltdown; in Beijing and Stockholm with Kung-Fu masters; at tango parlors in Buenos Aires; at temples in India; in Tahrir Square with a million Egyptians...

Hassett's life has been an unceasing and courageous half-century of philosophical inquiry, civil disobedience, defiance of existing socio-political structures, flagrant rebellion, and pursuit of the Real, of which this -- his first in a series of forthcoming volumes -- can attest. It is a fine and significant addition to the art of poetry.

Erin Currier 2012

Gazette

1

I saw the heart that roots you
In your restless circuit,
Arroyos where in dead puddles
One expects to find the deft
Remains of the flesh, or seasons…
Blood that tempers you, enfold
This tarn of departed weather,
That which scabbed over
When the merciless insomnia
Gave to the day ravages of whiteness,
Something essential, hole where humiliation's
Wound pulled toward a void
We could never fill…unreachable margin:
I too wanted you
To twist the muscle of our sweet
Musical tongue, but you were already
On your way, moving into the devastated
Sangre de Christo. And more:
More the heart that gives back an abrupt
Return to this tenable hell,
You narrate the rise and fall
Of our soft, vulnerable bodies
From the inferno below…

2

If in my heart there remains
Something of your broken promise
Then let the hour now striking
Be the hour of its apocalypse...
In the midst of dense
Lowering clouds scatter then
These omens, or show
In a flash of apparent flame,
The dear, monstrous transparencies
Of your hand...

As in distances, awakening
The imperceptible threat of yet
Another larval season-
We feel our incubus lift
And surround us, and...take heart:
Already the summer heat descends,
The sham image as it sparkles
And the water gall, burst...

If, in my heart, there remains
Something of that sordid mendacity,
Unknotting itself, released from the shrill...

3

Whenever you come back, close to me,
I feel the utter sadness
Of two bodies struggling to stay
The slope at their feet...this sheer
Of blind purposes has no need,
It forces upon us a return to the dreadful
Shuddering of the heart -in danger-
Agonies of the senses where
There is absolutely no sense,
Only the place where the flesh
Makes its pretense of passage,
Always an uneasy stillness
And isolate minutes passing too. In tender forms;
Not the splendor of the earth's tormented surfaces.
One wrenching, another gust,
A groan of explosions shall divide us from
What consolation? And after that,
What unfamiliar skies?
So world extends beauty against
Our dumb defense, and puts fear in the pulse
Where love should live, when comfort
For a moment could capture here...

4

Now an upsurge and the wind
Enters the garden, passes through the dark
Iron gate… you and I will not lose
One moment of this, as we are inheritors
Of the history of that breath, that phantom
Who bears life through us in such
Subtle threads.
For us, the World exists, is here,
And we are part of these used-up
Mortal acts that straddle
Both the foul and empyrean,
This is to say, anyone who breathes…

Perhaps with this earthly sign
Something of you is finally revealed.
And yet the leaf stalled mid-air
Traces only the shuddering ferment,
It offers nothing of your inexhaustible secret,
And nothing less -Maybe it's true;
Maybe you are the involuntary source,
Perpetual agitation
And point where all troubles join…

Or perhaps it is you who yields
This noxious and palpable breeze
Of voyant pain that, today,
Delivers its blow mid-heart…

5

Now that it is always night
These my separate pools of darkness
Leech edges of shade,
Now that your eyes have closed
Even these hours of inviolable distance
Rouse...divide me to you forever.

Again I touch your trusting hands.
But your sorrow makes use of me
In ways I cannot touch. If, out of agony,
You must raise me up, raise me to the stable
And firm above, or floor with lightning
These places...

Already autumn unflowers all that pleases
And leaves that which hurts or falls
For the eye's menacing graces.
My blindness is bright but your space
Reduced   -Even this flesh perishing,
These shadows vanishing... and you,
Casting some moment in the shock of exposure...

6

The sky is clouded over
And brutal winds
Roil the waters
There in the scrap
Of the bridges.
Except this single thing
With which need has bound me
Servile, a greater wind tears
Stone by stone, my strength,
And with half-closed eyes
Caught over the passing, as a shade,
I make sight of you…I see you conjured
At the length of the quay.

And my heart grows calm on the blue
Of that shore…impalpable
When high seas and winds
Drown out the gentle image
Of the world's end…

Dying, one into the other, where only eye
Might reach…your simple breath and chaos, dear.

7

With the violet
Tinted shadows of the willows
And this, amid the crosses
Of our cemetery...
 Evening coming on.
I recall you in complete mirage,
Your nude body sun-bathed through
The window; but what I thought
Sweet to dream
Is only to remember...in a sad time,
What used to be beautiful,
Other beings,
At that moment awake -My love,
Now all I ask from heaven from this oblivion
Is to be alive again,
And kiss you, my dead...

8

Silence and the sun so clear
I sought clover where I could find
Only thorn and salt...
But for the knowing of those nervous
Coils of ore, menacing carbons would set
Me back or snare where farther down sheers
Anthropos, shut in on itself
Like an unborn child...
Where the quiet laurel breathes in these
Hard dry hillsides, untouchable,
This little bit of wind, this small spun
Bloom of violets, and unsure fingers
Made suddenly sure.
And of all the ends, that end.
And of all the hours to pass away
Let this one's lulls be rarer still.
And your tenderness, too: the slow
Shade, the piece of suffering
Torn out of us by other beings,
The clover that even you might believe
Motive enough, for an instant
Of bright enchanted heat...

9

More between the shores where
Evening was a rumor of two hands
Clasped in a lifetime's gesture…
You, between and beneath, while others
Browsed on a darkness laved by dull
Drowsing…a disaster from the outset, your succubus
Glides by woods and narrows,
Company to those who delude and who bind
To another dream…

They are divine. And despite reversals
Their gesture remains. They measure out
An imprisonment of afterlife architecture,
Fleabag hereafters, into which the new soul throws blood,
Muscle, lymph -immersed in metaphorical embroideries,
Proud to murder.

We fear. Tempted to issue
Only the margins of our own nature
And to dwell on you, inverse.
Withdraw to the sound of bells and let
The police disperse these extra hours; already
Each new moment fends off a dying
Sweetness, while you are received
By another toll…

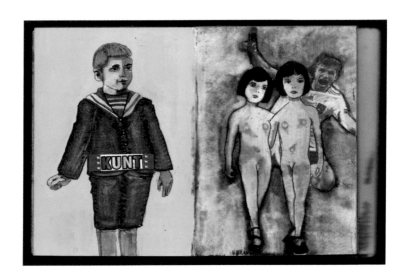

10

So when alone I still know
Splendid dreams, whole dreams
Even after years accompanied
By loss, defeat; here, even the one
Evening born of the womb is affixed
To inexpressible null and slow
Fatigue...
Yet is the moment when I lift
An astonished weight,
I bear alone above you the round
Occult moment that is
In no part an instant of this
Sickened life. Again I am
Sight dispersing your memory
In bursts of abdominal blood and light,
Mortal reminiscence and then
(If so) the force which guides you down.

11

You separate me from the peace
Of sleep, since in darkness
Your terror vexes, pulls…

And that which opens worlds to others
Leaves us enduring. You pray:
What is the word which opens
Every side, which way the fall
To a bright, level place,
And what illustration remains
To floor the void?

Leaning, a night is left angled
Against us… dark with sham starlight
It serves to gouge at the mind
In place of truces, spells…

12

Again, within me, and you
Turn to ascend another semblance
Where a shadow has doubled enough
To be mistaken...
Once more you shift in appearance
To trouble again our troubled time.

Surely the sound that led me deeper
Into dream, is yours, is accompanied
By your cry alone...
What you make of us I shall keep
And I shall keep it through your just
Measure, where now is scattered
My every breath.

Where, only moments past,
Your mouth was caught in the dumb
Struggle of a kiss –almost human-
And now the dead truly are
Killing the living, and through you
They receive with no other mystery
Than this, what is undone through form,
Form known only in flame...

13

Already you graze me...
Already halved you hang fire between us.
But for those lives which cannot speak,
Who rise from the ordinary curse, for them
The world darkens   -and this kingdom
Obliterates them, their human calm.
And you, you who seemed made of memory,
Incessant memory, you too would wear
The suit of material efflorescence,
But for the silver Latinity
Preceding you, this labor
Where the corpse grows transparent,
Porter of all spheres burned by material fire...

That you lift our earlier, now withered, poetry
To include pardon, love, memory
Content to evoke the past without regret,
For the sake of conjuring vermin, downfall...
Already your hand held up to fend away
Archons, standing apart from all human endeavor,
As higher than this day, maelstroms of dark
Ravines and ovens rage; as you have no doubt heard
The voice from that throat of chewed meat
And savage, assiduous wind; as you have seen
The great brazen hole blown clean
Through the poignant
Barricade...

14

When, returned to my mind,
An arc of pure ache more taut
Than any heart   -so I saw you.
And the sense of our absolute
Ending rushed forward to shatter
What little
Happy
Grace…as you have two delicate hands,
And yet one life retreats where,
Almost at once, your fingers gave birth
To dark clots of life,
This quick start that leaps up and away
From your touch.

And yet returned I still see
That street, our house, or remember
At your waist my anguished hands
Eclipsed…abysmal darkness that descends
Always on you, always on him.

15

Orchid, disaster, I know you...
We recall how the God's forehead
Opened, exposing the archaic
Machine that engraves
Curlicues on the backs of slaves...
How now and then
A white brine was discharged
From Jehovah's wart...
Comet
Coin
Kaiser,
Your two crippled wings
Enclose the central altarpiece
Acephalic.

Homelessness Begins at Home...

1

From the World

A heel is not a hammer
But whatever fulfills
The function of a god
Is a God.
I feel, when you sleep beside me,
The touch of your familiar breath
On my mouth.
It is in this place
Where, through some concentration
Of emptiness,
That ghosts are changed into men...

2

Bordercrossings

At Termini I caught
The train to Milano.
In that hour prior to departure
I remembered our
Final moments together.
Sleep, black and lifeless;
I edge back to the surface
Of the heavy earth.
What to think of those
Rough mountains near our home
Wrapped in chain-link,
The elephant-headed god Ganesh,
The crimped wire and whittled
Wood of a birdcage
Trampled...

3

Pallas Athena

Machine for seeing. Machine
For hearing. Once upon a time
Machine for thinking. In Berlin
We were wished good morning
By a riot…in Athens
One pile of burning garbage
Turned out to be -three bankers.
But in the ship away from Athens
I fell asleep, I dreamed of Kafka
And I remembered my forbearers
Drinking shit from the Austro-
Hungarian glass. Smack!
The long day doubled,
The gigantic, blind apparatus
Bared the device by doubling
The double, and from a generation's
Loins you spun both cell and stall,
The 3x3 arrest cages
Of brackets, clamps…

4

Foul Weather

Midwinter on Santorini, exhaustion
Counterfeiting quiet…in Brussels our great
Alexander comported himself like a pig;
Now dead, he is revered
For his large meaty porkers,
Legendary for his fine, even supernatural
Texture and flavor…
Once we took the luxurious stretch
To Thera…but when our horse stumbled
As we crossed the water,
A voice whispered from the shadows,
A Roman would have turned back…
They say the gift blesses the giver.
When we sought fame in Europe
Germany had not yet set her vermillion terms.
We saw the great Viking Northman, afraid of winter,
Afraid of violence, sweep through Athens

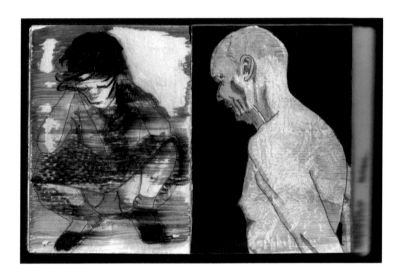

For weekend swaths of imperial purple;
Tired of cleaning fish...now perilously tired
Of banking and the swagger of shopping,
He flees, either to the Rhineland
Or the buckled knarrs of Iceland.
Midwinter...each season scraps the social hope;
Anchored in the dirty third-rate hole
Of sick, upchucking sensation,
Our great wheels of meat languish,
Each gorge and intestine in grotesque bustle,
And taste for the gothick
Philhellene, incarnadine seas...

5

Stone Trough

I return to that road in Chile,
Running like a bruised ribbon
Along an underbite of jagged
Stone incisors, down the cinder slope:
Back to India -Paravati's womb,
A tantric volcano in a pool
Of milk or sperm...your heated body
Pressed up against me in the taxi;
Through the light cloth your scent
Crowded out the scent of an entire country,
The warm crepe, the flame-red
Flowering world that quivered
Among the fine leaves, granite clouds
And the breeze. I remember now
As night fell we crept out of the hills
Into Iquique, where the moon
Cast its trash, garbage, waste
On bauxite mansions cloaked in vultures...

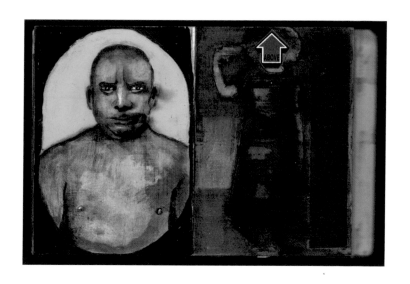

6

Debris

Sand dunes, a few creosote
Storms, landmines,
Piles of salt-rock covered
In blue tarp...
Girls carve up animals
In a stall near
A brightly painted
Clapboard shack;
The stench of roast pig,
The sight of white flesh
Growing crisp and brown,
Fat turning yellow and oozing oil,
Hissing as it pools in the glowing coals...
In Rio de Janiero, chauffeured helicopters
Ferry businessmen over a seashore
Of demolished huts
To dine on "one fish split in half,
Pan fried and tossed on a plate
With raw onion, tomato -one hundred Euros."
On the street below two men argue
Over whether a woman's uterus floats freely
Inside the body, unless anchored by a fetus,
A parentheses enclosing the always
Already animal voice of death...

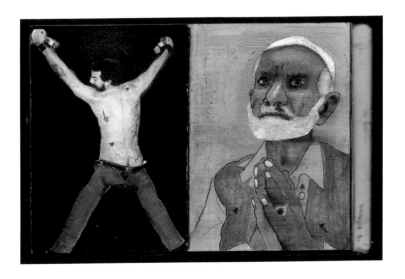

7

Humanoid

Someone
Swings the name of Jesus
Up from the dirt.
But even Jesus
Was out of his depth
Here, like a fisherman
At his first fire.

Here
The wind pushes the trees
All one way
And every building
Is a ruin.
Little girls on the corners
Sway gently.
The dark hilltops
Of the city
Roar.

Here
We will die
Of our surroundings,
As brutal as any paddock.
The girls on the corners
Lift their muzzles
For affection…

O let more war come
To clean these streets:

The children
Of the hanged
Are insolent
Still…

8

Emeth

Steadily we crossed the wilderness
Knowing at dawn the world
Would be gone. Stepping over
Those slumbering bodies
I felt the breeze carry me away
From that scorched aureole
Of ragged scrap… Mortal damage.
This world now deserted,
Its windows and doors
Sealed by metal grills…and massive
Stone boulders, charred black and splintered,
Arranged across the plains…

9

German Rhyme

Sunrise in hell; small wonder
We go screaming for cover.
Passing over the summer camps
And coffee shops and small hotels,
A shadow too large to gag
On plastic walks the sky
To annihilation. Now, when the door
Swings open we never know
What will come through it...
Second only to Rome under Caligula,
Second only to the strap-tight
Bed frame, "as if to harness a lunatic."

10

Mad Toll

Things were so bad I finally
Took refuge in the shrines
Of Sindh, soon joining the tantric
Witch at Tarapith...I returned then,
Sliding beneath the underpass
Of the Hollywood freeway,
Fleeing the trap in the landscape
Beneath Saturn's kerosene
Colored glass -our heaven, our Ama,
Our plump idol in the extravagant mansions
Off Beverly Glen...and gone
The white suburbs of Dharamsala, gone
The blunt nave of the Dalai
Lama's miraculous micro-Potola...
Only red earth lesions, bleeding arteries
That feed the old wattle stalls
And stables of sucking, translucent underlife...irregular trees,
The run-off from pelvic oracles
Blending human drainage, dry branches, dead leaves,
And the punitive Before/After
Dzogchen diptych
Coming at twilight...

11

Kokelstunde

The seaweed with its floatation
Bulbs and mannitol crystals,
The sky, such as it was, not much different
Than now, swarming with zeppelins
And clusters of fog galvanized by sunlight.
We had not yet become "Great,"
Our white power slid out from beneath
Our feet, homicidal but still brooding
Over the Aztec sundial at Manila, Oahu...
Until the first sortie
Smashed the ball past the park
Our Executive remained dull, content
To break the public trust with monologues.
Now endowed, inspired by impulse,
Accident throws up its subjects
And the plot swallows them.
A strip search, buttocks spread...and I worry
The world might be shrinking too fast...
 I fall asleep fearing
There might not be enough room
 For others to fuck off in...

12

September Eleven

There was so much methamphetamine
And sodomy, in the end
All the participants could do
Was cry...the pit bulls
Were put away, the bullhorn
Sounded in the street
But no one listened,
And it chanted as it took hold,
Cosseting the vast and monstrous
Dawn, it brought noise down
Around our ears,
Patting us like dogs...of course
The videos helped immeasurably
And the thought of one's own gaze
Being returned...the morning sunlight
Stretched out like a body
On a rack; fighter jets rushed overhead
And the wretched shape
Of runt luminescence

Bled the depth from our view…
In the end it was our own God-given
Visages -our disheveled hair,
Our manicured goatees,
The little gaps between our teeth,
Our full lips…in the end
There was the inscription
Of crimes committed, the heresies, expulsions.
As we may never know
The alam al mithal,
Or even tenderness.
After so many perjuries,
Who can sing the human song…too many years
Flying blind, too much worry
That God's eyes might have eyelids
After all…

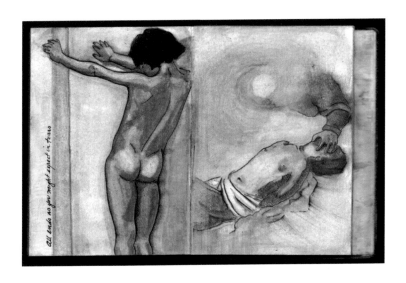

13

Round Graves

We remember those pagans
Who lived in the world
Prior to Christ, the damned
Of the earth who carved their names
In the mud of Brittany or the Massif Central,
Melancholy proper.... Whose hopes were crushed
In the revolution, and who held in their mind's eye
One birth breeched by a common
Bourgeois reality, while the other contained signs...

Here, it seems, our failed contact
Left among the dirty guts and garbage
A dismembered Tsar, Tsarina.... No man sleeps
With the same demon twice, no man skips out
For a night of "poetry", nor awakens
As naked and young as he was last week.
We think back to those first housebroken bodies,
How they carried, each to each, chipped pails
Billowing fire,
Who hung themselves dead in their own image
While the sewers of Harappa
Drained fire, Soma, fire, the river....

14

Heimat

We say prayers
For the ten years
Pecked to death
After the slaughter.
Now, in the third month out,
I'm astonished at the carnage.
But I remember reading something
Somewhere...
Never mind. If the words ran out
We would stay suspended here
In purgatorial, moonlit shade.
We would feel that overload of being
I believe, that we sometimes hear
Over the noise of harbored grudges,
That freedom from the hoax that walks
At an angle to the past tense, and worse...

15

In Cairo

Worsening civil war
Among warlords
And mujahedeen.
Scattered, they bury themselves
In a pig-farmer's field
Until NATO soldiers
Come to resurrect them.
Forty-eight years gone
And I look and act
Like a fool: where is
The moral glamour in rebellion?
In the wry existential puzzle
There are no matters
Of life and death.
Biting insects are disgorged
By the cold wind
Off the ice. Boreal forests
During eight or nine months
Of ice and blizzard
Are followed by a brief
Summer season of safe drilling.
A venomous snake will
Marshall himself to a single
Goal -but he won't strike in darkness.
He holds a piece of Man's
Heart in his heart,
And man a piece of snake...

Published by CSF Publishing, New Mexico, USA
Please visit csfpublishing.com